This book is dedicated to my wife, my sons,
the students I have instructed
and the prompting by them that

"I should write a book"

about my techniques and teaching methods
that have improved their golf games.

Introduction

As we age, our bodies change and we are not able to compete or play golf as in years past. Physical ailments, injuries, diminishment of strength and the natural aging process limit us in what we are able to do in the golf arena.

It is important that we be able to continue our pursuit of the game of golf and to increase our enjoyment in our later years. As a result, I have formulated an instruction program for use by Seniors that has returned positive results for both men and women. It relies on many of the principles and fundamentals that each of us were taught (or learned) in our earlier years.

This book will provide the basis for re-defining golf from a Seniors' perspective. It will provide a foundation to build upon and will "modify or rebuild" the golf swing for greater ease and enjoyment of the game. It may contain many items you are already familiar with and some that you may not have heard about or learned previously.

Ben Hogan wrote a book about the five fundamentals of the game of golf. It contains elements which he believed would assist every golfer in their quest for perfection. He was not only one of the best to ever play the game but was very insightful about the basics of the game. In this book you will recognize some of his teachings in addition to things that I have learned over the years and my teaching methods that have worked for golfers of all ages.

In this book you will find pictures and step by step instructions to assist you in playing the game of golf with proven practice routines that reinforce the fundamentals of the golf swing.

I sincerely hope that you will gain benefit from the instructional methods and techniques shown within the pages of this book.

Gary J. Lee PGA – Teaching Professional

Table of Contents

THE PRE-SHOT and SETUP ROUTINE

A solid pre-shot routine is the basis
for excelling in the sport.
It is the first step in creating a
"Repeatable" and "Consistent" swing.

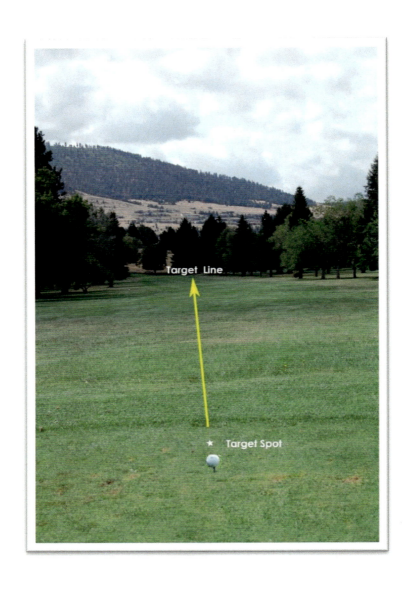

STEP 1 – Target Selection

THE FOUNDATION

Every good player has something in common. They all have a pre-shot or setup routine that provides a solid foundation from which they can swing the club with greater confidence. Repeating the pre-shot routine for every shot will provide the player with greater consistency, accuracy and provide necessary feedback on what may be happening during the swing process. This is the most important step for a senior golfer as it provides a solid foundation for what happens in the swing stage. (I will explain the swing feedback process later)

Step 1 – Your Target

Stand behind the ball and look at where you want the ball to go. Imagine a straight line from the ball to your desired target.

Select a spot (location) 1-4 feet in front of the ball and down the target line. This is the point where you will square up and align your golf club during the pre-shot routine.

Take one, two or three practice swings. When you "feel" the tempo being relaxed and the club almost swinging itself, then proceed with the setup. Remember ... the practice swing should be with tempo. Focus on tempo and you will be more prepared to relax and swing the club with less effort.

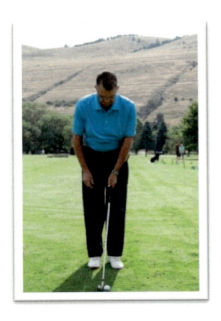 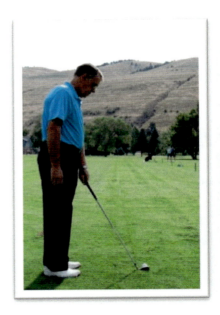

Step 2 …. Club Alignment – Iron

STEP 2 …. Club Alignment – Wood

Step 2 – Club Alignment

Move forward and face the ball. Place both feet together with the ball centered directly between your feet.

Next, place the club flat on the ground directly behind the ball. With the hand placed on the club, move the clubface right, left etc. until you square the clubface at 90 degrees to the target "spot" or line.

After so many years of playing golf, many seniors rely on what they have done in the past and forget the main principle for aligning the clubface to the target. Essentially, it is a 90 degree perpendicular line (from the center of the clubface) at which the ball will be directed down the target line when the club makes contact.

This is the most important part of the golf pre-shot routine! Aligning the clubface to the target! You will never direct the ball on the path that you have chosen without correctly aligning the clubface first.

Many of us get so used to just gripping the club and placing it behind the ball without thinking about the correct alignment. We set the club on the ground (like we have done hundreds of times before) and think we have it aligned correctly. Chances are ... the clubface is a little open or a little closed which will cause the ball to be off target.

Be very deliberate with this alignment routine. The more consistent the setup routine is ... the greater chance for straighter and more precise shots.

TYPICAL WOOD (with center mark)

TYPICAL IRON (without center mark)

IRON (with center mark)

Step 2 – Club Alignment to Ball Position

For consistency, ball flight and ball control, always make sure the ball is centered on the club face for every shot. This will reduce the number of toe or heel shots (off center strikes) during the swing process.

Most drivers and woods have a mark on the top of the club. This is where the "sweet spot" of the clubface is located and this point should always be aligned directly with the center of the ball.

Unfortunately, most irons do not have an alignment mark. As a method for determining the correct ball alignment for the irons, I will sometimes take a magic marker and place a mark on the top of the iron to assist in the alignment of the clubface to the ball. This will help to avoid those "toe" or "heel" shots as mentioned before.

The player must insure that the ball is centered on the clubface during the setup routine to increase the potential to obtain "solid" hits on the ball and to maximize performance and distance.

In drastic cases, I will scribe a mark on the top of the club indicating the clubface center and the "sweet spot" for the club.

It doesn't matter what you do, or how you do it, you must take every precaution to align the "sweet spot" of the clubface with the ball each time you setup to take a shot.

Our goal here is to become more consistent in each and every step of the setup process. Repeating these steps will lead to greater consistency on the golf course and better ball striking.

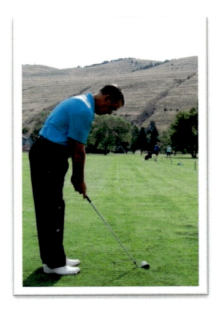

Step 3 – Bow to the Queen – Take your Iron Grip

Step 3 – Bow to the Queen – Take your Driver Grip

Step 3 – The Correct Posture

After you align the club along your target line you will then "bow to the queen" by bending at the waist with your arms pointing downward at the ground.

Feel this relaxed position. The back is straight, knees slightly bent and there is no tension in your arms and chest areas.

This position is optimal for the golf swing and will automatically align your shoulders, chest, hips and knees along your target line.

Check to see that your weight is evenly distributed between the heels and toes of your shoes. If you feel more weight on your toes you will be "reaching" for the ball. If you feel more weight on your heels you are standing too close to the ball.

The adjustment of your weight is very important so that your setup position is optimized. I cannot stress this point enough. Once you have completed this step you should feel comfortable and relaxed.

You then proceed to placing your grip on the club.

Baseball or 10 Finger Grip

Interlocking Grip (baby and index fingers interlocked)

Overlap Grip (baby finger rests on top)

Step 4 – The Grip

While "bowing to the queen" - carefully take your grip (very lightly) with the clubface aligned to your target line and the butt of the club pointing at your navel.

The grip must be comfortable for each individual player regardless of their age or playing ability. The type of grip doesn't matter. It can be an interlocked, overlap, or the ten finger baseball grip.

Take your grip by placing your forward hand (left hand for righties and right hand for lefties) on the club with the grip resting in the last three fingers of your forward hand. Move your thumb forward or back on the top of the grip until the grip rests comfortably in the last three fingers. This is very important. It is the step where you insure that the hand is securely placed on the grip in the correct position. Place the other hand on the grip. Now relax the hands. There shouldn't be any tension in your forearms or with the grip. If there is … just lower your hands slightly towards the ground until you feel completely relaxed.

It has been my experience that most golfers grip the club too tightly which creates tension and stress in the hands, arms and even the chest. The grip should be relaxed but firm. Check yours by taking your grip and extending the club to waist high. Have another person pull the club towards them. You should be able to feel your hands lightly on the grip and the club slightly moving forward and back. If you are "pulled" forward your grip is too tight. Loosen it until you can barely "feel" the club moving. This will be the proper pressure for your grip.

STEP 5 – IRON POSITION (middle of stance)

STEP 5 – DRIVER POSITION (forward in stance)

Step 5 – Ball Positioning and Stance

Now that we have your club and body aligned target we are ready to set our stance. Remember always adjust your stance to the ball position.

To set your stance ... your feet should be approximately shoulder width apart for irons and slightly wider for woods and the driver.

1. For irons .... Set your stance equally with the ball position in the middle (or slightly forward) of center.

2. For the driver .... Set your stance by moving your left foot approximately 1" – 2" forward and towards your target. Then set your rear foot. When you are in the proper position, the ball should be slightly forward and inside of the leading foot.

As we age, a seniors' flexibility and agility diminishes over a period of time. It is more difficult to make a complete shoulder turn or complete the hip rotation as in the past which results in a loss of distance.

There is a simple method for assisting in the turn process by slightly rotating the toes of the feet outward which greatly enhances your ability to turn more freely. Try this by taking your normal stance then (leaving your heel in place) rotate the toe slightly outward.

Remember to always adjust (set) your stance to the club and the ball. Too many golfers walk up to the ball gripping the club prior to going through a pre-shot routine. In doing so they position the clubface open or closed and the result will be a "push", "pull", "fade" or "hook".

Driver Focus:

At the completion of your setup routine your eyes should be focused on the point at which the tee enters the ground.

This will insure that your weight has partly shifted to your rear foot just prior to beginning the swing process.

Iron Focus:

At the completion of your setup routine your eyes should be focused on the point at which the ball touches the ground.

This will insure that your weight has partly shifted to your rear foot just prior to beginning the swing process.

Step 6 – Final Setup Position

In years past we were able to setup and shift our weight to the rear and then move it to the front side during the swing process. As seniors, we want to make a simpler transition.

To accomplish this, try to position your weight on your rear foot to begin every shot. Begin shifting your weight to your rear foot by looking downward and forward to the bottom ¼ of the ball (on the ground) for irons or, at the point where the tee goes into the ground for the driver. Your rear shoulder should go down slightly and you should feel the weight shifting at this point to the inside of your rear foot to begin the swing process. **Keep it there!** It will automatically transition forward during the swinging of the club and your hip rotation. The weight transfer will be a lot simpler and one less thing to worry about.

You have now completed the basic setup via the pre-shot routine. Once your routine is set …. **FORGET** about it and move to the next step.

Note: *the benefits and results of a good pre-shot routine are numerous. Your shoulders' waist and knees will be in alignment with your target; you will be in a better and more relaxed position to swing the club; the clubface will be squared and directed along your target line; you have a consistent starting point for each and every time you get ready to swing the club; It will assist you greatly in producing a repeatable swing; and most importantly, your confidence will increase in knowing your setup is the foundation for everything else that will happen during the swing process.*

One Piece Take-Away

Preparation for the Swing - The club take away, swing tempo and length of backswing is your next focus.

Remember … Have only one swing thought! Don't stand over the ball for long periods of time. Once you have completed the pre-shot routine, think of one swing thought and swing the club with confidence. Back off and start over if you feel any tension or hesitation in what you want to do.

One of my favorite sayings: *"There is no ball in the game of Golf. It just gets in the way of a good swing."*

If your focus is on the ball you will try to "hit at it". Try thinking about making a good swing and letting your club work for you. If you think swing - the clubface will strike the ball and direct it down the target line in a more consistent manner.

Here are some of the swing thoughts to consider: Low and slow take away; tempo; rotate hips; grip pressure; relax; finish the shot etc.

Remember …. Only one swing thought at a time.

One Piece Take-Away

Left shoulder, one piece "take away" creates leverage and promotes greater distances and consistency. Think of leverage as an integral part of the swing. Physics tells us that a longer lever decreases the effort required to move an object. In golf … the object is the ball. The lever begins at the shoulder extends through our arms and the length of the club. If you break your wrists or bend your elbow it reduces the effective length of the lever thus limiting distance and control at the point of your club making contact with the ball.

Shorten the Backswing for Better Tempo

Swing Tempo

I always emphasize Tempo, Tempo and more Tempo. This assists in creating the "marshmallow" effect. You know ... "that feeling" when your swing is effortless and the ball just "takes off" and you say "wow".

Picture an equal swing movement of the club – both backward and forward. Feel a smooth transition from the backswing to the downswing. Sometimes it may help your swing tempo if there is a momentary pause transitioning from the backswing to the downswing.

As senior golfer's we are no longer capable of making that "big turn" as in our younger years. So why try? Think about taking a half swing. Focus on a shorter swing with better tempo. It will produce better shots and improve your swing process.

Many seniors try to regain their former yardage by over swinging the club. This is the worst thing you can possibly do. Your body and muscles must move in concert with each other. Use your hip rotation and tempo to create distance.

Remember the length of your backswing determines the basis for your tempo – not speed. Remember ... low and slow club head take away for your irons, woods and putter.

RELAX! For every swing to have a positive effect you must relax completely prior to initiating the swing. Some of my students will take a deep breath and then blow it out immediately prior to taking the club back. Others will "waggle" the club loosely in their hands which also eliminates tension.

One Piece - Take-Away

Backswing – Left Arm Horizontal

The Swing Itself

First of all, consider the swing as the most important element of the game once you have mastered the setup with the pre-shot routine. The swing should feel natural, not rushed or herky-jerky but a smooth take-away which transitions from the top of your back swing to the downswing to your finish position without a lot of effort.

Most of my senior students utilize the "one-piece" take-away as mentioned previously. It is more controlled and assists in transferring weight to the rear foot.

It begins by starting the backswing with the shoulder, arm and the wrists working in conjunction to form a "long" lever. The club is pushed backward and low to the ground then upwards to a position where your left arm is horizontal with the ground and you have a "natural" and limited wrist break. When doing this move, notice how your weight has transferred to the rear foot. This move eliminates excess body slide and club head rotation which assists in returning the club to the correct impact position with the ball during the swing process.

I cannot stress this enough - do not over swing! It is one of the most common faults for golfers of all ages and especially for seniors. It can cause a disruption of tempo … your arms, elbow, and hands get too high during the backswing which adversely affects the entire swing process and you will most likely "rush" the downswing. I guarantee you that your shots will not be what you might anticipate or expect.

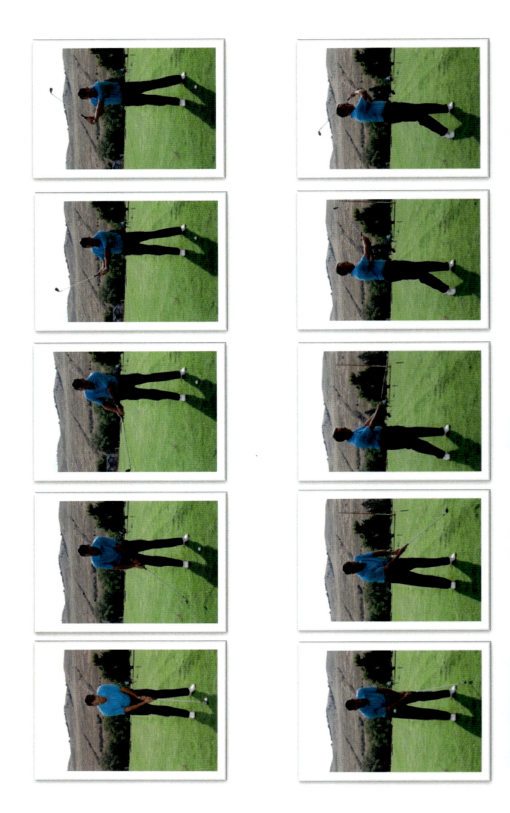

To begin the downswing you must rotate the hips <u>first</u> with your weight remaining on your rear foot and transitioning to the front foot during the swing. This move will start the right elbow moving to your side with the arms and club coming downward to contact the ball.

<u>Do not move or slide your hips forward and then turn the hips. This will increase the likelihood that the clubface will be open at the point of impact which will produce a slice or push.</u>

Finish the shot by completing the downswing and turning so your navel is facing the target and the club is skyward. (See correct finish position)

For senior players, I always stress the importance of accelerating the club through the point of impact with good tempo. Let the shaft and the club "work" for you. <u>Remember that "the ball only gets in the way of a good swing".</u>

Again ... remember to only have one swing thought. It could be tempo, the one piece take-away, weight back on rear foot, lower your hands, lighten your grip, length of backswing, breathing, relax or whatever helps you to get ready for the shot.

The more practice you get ... the more comfortable you will become with the process. You will begin to eliminate extra "thoughts" one by one until you settle in with the correct swing thought given the situation.

With practice (and by utilizing these techniques) your swing and tempo should improve dramatically. If you experience difficulties with your tempo, timing and balance, use the practice drills as shown in the practice techniques and drills section.

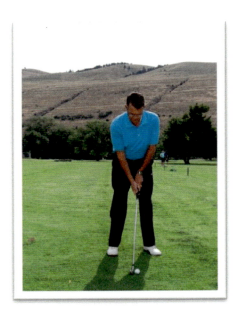

Iron Setup – Ball in Middle of Stance

Hybrid and Wood Setup – Ball Forward in Stance

Hybrids, Driver and Fairway Woods

The latest technologies in Hybrid Irons have greatly enhanced the ability of senior golfers to have more solid strikes on the ball with greater consistency. Hybrid irons are easier to swing then the customary longer irons. They can be used under varying circumstances. Be it on the fairway, in the rough and even for bunker play.

The same can be said for the Driver and Fairway Woods. New designs allow the senior golfer to adjust the club for a specific swing pattern. It can be made to draw or fade and most have an adjustable loft feature. When adjusted correctly, the launch angle (the angle at which the ball flies off the clubface) reduces backspin which allows for greater distances. The adjustable settings for a draw or fade can compensate for the swing path (outside in or inside out) that the senior golfer might have. These adjustments assist in creating a straighter shot with longer distances.

Hybrid and Driver Swing Differences

It has been my observation teaching senior golfers that the new technological equipment greatly enhances the golf experience. The clubs are easier to hit from the fairways and out of the rough.

However, the major difference is in swinging the golf club. The setup is the same as irons except for the ball position. (see pictures) The second biggest difference is that the swing itself is more of a sweeping motion instead of down and thru.

Modify your preshot routine to stand slightly taller after taking your stance. Adjust your shoulders back with the rear shoulder slightly down. My senior students have had good success by utilizing this specific setup addition.

The Swing Feedback Process

Helping students understand what has transpired in a previous shot will provide a greater understanding of where a swing problem may exist. For example … the ball may go right or left, it may slice or hook, the ball was hit thinly or fat, the trajectory wasn't what you expected; the distance was either longer or shorter than what you planned. You ask yourself what would cause that to happen?

This is where feedback comes into play. If you can feel it, see it or hear it - you are halfway to understanding the problem. A basic understanding of physics, geometry and mathematics will certainly assist in this process.

Ask yourself what causes the ball to do certain things?

- o Why did I slice or hook the ball?
- o Why did it go low?
- o Why did I hit it fat?

All these questions (and many more) will arise at some point in time. The senior golfer needs to understand the importance of "knowing" their own swing. This comes from playing and practicing while focusing on specific areas of the setup and the swing.

I like to explain reasons why certain things happen so that the student can learn the causes, are aware of what just happened, and be able to correct the shot the next time they are in the same situation. This is commonly referred to as "cause and effect".

Some common effects and their causes:

The ball slices –
- The stance is "too" open
- The swing path is outside to inside
- The clubface is open when striking the ball
- The hands are underneath the grip and not turning over
- The hands are forward and ahead of the clubface at impact
- The elbow slides past the side of the body
- The hips slide forward before rotating

The ball hooks –
- The stance is closed
- The swing path is inside to outside
- The clubface is closed when striking the ball
- The hands have over rotated
- The weight remains on the back foot and didn't transfer

The trajectory is lower than expected -
- The hands are slightly ahead of, and leading, the clubface
- The weight is on the front foot
- The clubface is "shut down" at point of impact
- The ball position is in the back of the stance
- The club descends on the ball at too steep of an angle

All of these situations can lead to additional strokes on the course. See the practice drills section for cures to some of these common problems.

PUTTING, CHIPPING and PITCHING
is at least 50%
of most SENIORS games.

Your practice should reflect equal time
devoted to this part of your game.

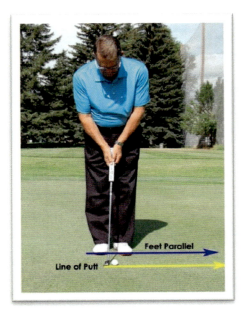

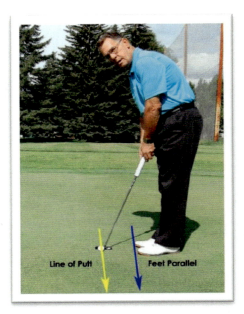

Square Alignment – Front

Square Alignment – Side

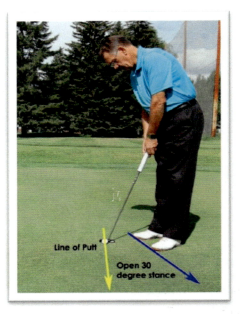

Open Alignment – Front

Open Alignment – Side

Putting:

Another one of my favorite sayings: *"Low and slow – right hand in the hole."* This forces you to accelerate through the ball and provides feedback as to the length of backswing taken for specific distances.

The putting stance is "what feels comfortable for you". Many senior golfers putt with an "open" alignment to eliminate any hip movement in the stroke and it positions them so that they can "see" the putting line more clearly.

An "open alignment" is where the front foot is placed slightly rearward and forward of the trailing foot. Many others prefer the square alignment where both feet are parallel to the putting line.

Your preference is what is most important. Remember to place the majority of your weight on your forward foot. Your stance should be comfortable no matter if it is open or squared.

The right hand is the dominate hand for putting right-handed. The left hand should be passive and just "lay" over the right without any pressure being applied. The back of the left hand should always be pointing in the direction of your putting line.

Remember *"Low and slow – right hand in the hole."* Take the club back slowly, slightly pause and then accelerate the clubface forward and along your intended target line. "Feel" the right hand directing the club straight back and straight forward on your target line.

Most of my students have improved their putting and decreased their putts per round by using this technique.

Putting Grips

Conventional   **Cross Handed**   **Tour Modified**

There are numerous styles of putting grips. It seems like every day a new one emerges from the players on the PGA and LPGA tours. We, as seniors, will see the various types of grips on the television and in magazines and try them in an effort to improve our scoring. A few are shown above on this page.

The fact of the matter is ... every player (senior or not) is always searching for a better and more consistent approach to their putting. It could be the size or style of the putter grip, the putter itself, their setup or alignment, the putting stroke or any number of other factors.

Today's putter designs are plentiful in the marketplace. A player should like the "look" and "feel" of the putter to improve their confidence. Rather than modify the type of grip or their position and setup, a number of my students have opted for purchasing a new putter in hopes that their scoring will improve. Sometimes it works and other times it doesn't.

Remember it is always the archer and not the arrow.

Speed (pace) versus line (direction)

Throughout time the question of line versus speed has been debated and which one is more important? I believe that each and every putt is different and it really depends on the situation.

For example … is it more important to have the correct speed on a downhill putt or have the right "read" (line)?

Would you rather have the ball go past the hole or stop short of the hole (speed) or not break as you had imagined (the line)?

I personally believe it is a combination of both. If I had to select one versus the other I would have to say that speed (distance) is more important for uphill and downhill putts and line is more important on sidehill or breaking putts.

Reading Greens

Think of water drainage. How would water on the green flow off the putting surface? It always drains from the high point to the low point.

Look for drainage areas around the green. Many greens are sloped from the back to the front for drainage purposes. Slower uphill and faster downhill putts are the result.

For undulating greens, look at the point at which a putt will fall directly to the hole. Where is the target point (the high side) of the ridge? Find this point and it will give you an idea as to how much break (curve) there is in the putt.

The Setup

The Take-Away

The Finish

Ball – Off Toe Position

Ball – Off Instep Position

Ball – Center Position

Chipping and Pitching

This section is where seniors' can usually improve their game and scoring average.

The thought process is simple … attempt to duplicate your putting stroke with your wedges for pitching and chipping the ball. For longer shots … increase the length of the backswing and follow through on every shot with the club head pointing to the hole. This will insure that you accelerate through the ball and along your desired swing path.

The process

Open your stance and place your weight on your left side (right handed players) with your hands slightly forward. Take a backswing with the club low to the ground. Then, begin the forward swing visualizing the target and swing the club through the ball and finish with the club pointing at the target.

Start practicing with the ball in the back of your stance and experiment with the ball position by moving it forward in the stance. You will begin to realize some differences that it will make in the ball flight, stopping and ball "roll out". The forward ball position promotes a higher trajectory and softer landing whereas the rear position has a lower trajectory and rolls farther after landing.

Practice from 15 yards, 25 yards, 30 yards etc. and develop the one tempo swing for chips and putts.

In rough or long grass … Think taking the club "up" (more steeply) and then hit "down" just behind the ball.

Approach Shots to the Green

For years I have advocated a controlled swing when hitting these types of shots. Great success and shot consistency has been obtained by utilizing this technique. Not only is it viable for approach shots to a green but, it can also be used for shorter shots on par 3's.

Begin by selecting the next higher club for the shot distance. For example …. If it would be a 9 iron shot … take out the 8 iron. Choke down on the grip ½" – 1". Begin setting up by using your pre-shot routine. The ball position should be slightly <u>back</u> of the center position. Your stance should be slightly open and your hands pressed slightly forward. Your weight should also be slightly forward.

Practice swinging the club easily and controlled with a shorter ½ or ¾ backswing. Find the tempo that you are comfortable with and is repeatable. Make sure that your swing "finish" position is the same as a full swing shot. You should feel the right hand directing the clubface to the target.

Find your average distances by hitting your pitching wedge several times with the swing tempo and shorter backswing that you have practiced. Mark the yardage down. Repeat this with your 9 iron, 8 iron and 7 iron.

Practice this on the range to develop consistency and confidence. Take it to the course and utilize it. You will experience greater results with your approach shots without the need to take "full" swings from shorter distances.

The next time you watch a tournament on TV … note how many players <u>don't</u> take a full shot from closer distances to the green. Ever wonder why? Consistency and shot control is the reason.

RATING AND SLOPE: BLACK 73.5/139 GOLD 71.1/133 SILVER M 68.0/119 L 73.6/127 BRONZE M 65.2/113 L 69.9/119

HOLE	1	2	3	4	5	6	7	8	9	OUT	10	11	12	13	14	15	16	17	18	IN	TOT	HCP	NET
BLACK	390	591	442	182	400	384	489	223	444	3545	379	625	422	238	442	361	534	166	431	3598	7143		
GOLD	371	561	416	161	377	349	459	181	400	3275	358	580	398	203	385	342	511	139	399	3315	6590		
SILVER	333	511	378	130	332	320	432	154	363	2953	312	528	384	169	361	308	453	122	351	2988	5941		
BRONZE	294	474	338	96	305	291	392	116	318	2624	275	450	320	124	320	265	405	108	325	2592	5216		
HANDICAP M	13	7	3	17	11	5	1	15	9		8	6	10	16	2	12	4	18	14				
Joan	4 X*	6 X	5 X	4 *	6 X	4 X*	4	5 *	5 X*	43 6X 5*	5 X*	6 X	5 X*	3 *	4 X	4 X*	6 X*	3 *	4 X*	40 7X 6*	83 13X 11*		
Putts	2	1	2	3	3	2	1	4	3	21	3	1	3	2	1	2	1	2	2	17	38		
Penalties												ob											
PAR	4	5	4	3	4	4	5	3	4	36	4	5	4	3	4	4	5	3	4	36	72		
Doug	5 X*	5 X	4 X*	4 *	4 X	5 X*	5 X	3 *	4 X*	40 7X 6*	4 X*	5 X*	5 X	3 *	4 X	5 X*	5 *	3 *	5 X*	39 6X 5*	79 13X 11*		
Putts	3	1	3	3	1	3	1	2	2	19	2	1	2	2	1	3	1	2	3	17	36		
Penalties			haz																				
HANDICAP L	11	9	5	17	13	3	1	15	7		12	8	14	18	6	2	4	16	10				

MARKER

DATE

PLAYER

48

Your expectations

A professional golfer hits fairways and greens in regulation approximately 65%-75% of the time. They earn millions of dollars on tour with these results. They practice and play almost every day for weeks at a time.

As a senior golfer (man or woman) **what are your expectations?** Are two, or perhaps three, out of ten shots acceptable? Do you practice for an hour or so each week and play perhaps two or three times a month?

Always be realistic in your goals. Many of us have sustained injuries, had health problems and lost mental focus over the years? Ask yourself - what is your true potential? What do you do well? What needs work? What are you unable to do? Ask yourself these questions and then create a positive mental attitude and you will begin to see an improvement in practice, in playing and in enjoyment of the game.

My philosophy is simple. Your expectations and focus should be positive ... If the ball moves closer to the target and your next shot is shorter than your last shot to the target then ... forget about it and move to the next shot. It doesn't matter what you did before - the important thing is what you will do next!

By using the techniques in this book you should begin to see an improvement in ball striking, direction and distance control. In addition, if you focus on the shot at hand and forget the poor shots of the past you will dramatically improve your focus concentration and consistency.

EXERCISING FOR GREATER PERFORMANCE

or NOT!

Exercising

There are many books written on this subject over the years. I do not pretend to be an expert in this field however; I would strongly suggest that every senior golfer research this subject thoroughly prior to undertaking a regime or routine for strengthening your muscles used in the game of golf. Consult a professional trainer and your primary physician prior to initiating a program of this type.

I would also like to point out that recent studies have shown that stretching exercises prior to playing golf may actually be harmful to your body. Stretching elongates specific muscles but must be held for a duration of 7 seconds or more to have any positive effect. Some stretching exercises may actually inhibit the swing motion and body movement.

I advocate "warming up" rather than stretching prior to playing a round of golf. This is proven (by physical therapy studies and observation of my students) to be a method that will enhance the golf experience and not be harmful to the body. It is simply swinging the club slowly forward and backward with tempo. This will get your golf muscles working and loosened up.

The first step in exercising is to realize that we, as seniors, have less flexibility and less strength than in years past. How do we gain strength? The answer quite simply is to exercise more often and in the correct manner.

How to we improve our flexibility? How do we prepare for a round of golf? These are the two questions we should be asking ourselves.

Warming up before play – Irons and Woods

At some point in time, every one of us have gone to the golf course and went straight to the tee box without hitting range balls or "warming up." We've felt "tight" and swing the club a couple of times to loosen up immediately prior to hitting that first shot.

Then what do we do? Do we swing hard or do we slow the swing down? Generally seniors will attempt the shot by swinging the club with a slower tempo to promote a more consistent and desirable shot.

Using this thought process and approach I strongly support the following techniques that each of us should be using on the driving range to warm up prior to playing.

- o Start slow by swinging a short iron (with one hand) forward and backward simulating a relaxed swing while rotating your hips during the back swing and the forward swing.
- o Begin with ½ swings then ¾ swings in a very relaxed motion. Feel a pendulum movement, both backwards and forward. Easy does it. Don't try to take a complete swing. Just relax and swing back and forth until your rhythm feels comfortable.
- o Take your hybrid, fairway wood or driver and repeat the ½ and ¾ swing process.
- o Once you begin to feel relaxed you can begin your pre-shot and setup routine by selecting a pitching wedge, 9 iron, 8 iron etc. to begin your warm up.
- o Make ½ swing shots and progressively elongate the swing to ¾ for several more shots. When the swing begins to feel comfortable and relaxed ... keep swinging it until it "really" feels right to you and you

have confidence with your club impact and the direction and flight of the ball.

- o Begin taking a full swing with the selected club – remember the arm should be across your chest and horizontal with the ground at the top of your backswing. Think of rhythm and smooth swings.
- o Gradually go from a short iron to a mid-iron then to your hybrids, fairway woods and finally your driver. Repeat the above process for each selected club. You do not have to hit every club in your bag! You are only warming up.
- o I have found that this "warm up" method works extremely well for senior golfers and promotes the flexibility of the body and enhances the actual swing process.

Warming up before play – Chipping and Putting

These two elements of the game are primarily based on "feel". Your purpose in the pre-round practice should be to develop some form of comfort level (feel) for this part of your game prior to going out to play.

Remember that a chip. pitch or putting stroke counts the same as that long drive. Keeping this in mind, be more deliberate with your short game to make up for any poor shots you may have had prior to reaching the green.

Begin your practice by chipping the ball from varying distances to a target. Develop your swing tempo and comfort level.

Take this tempo and relaxed feeling to the putting green. Line up and putt the ball to the hole. Get a sense of the speed. (see chipping and putting practice drills)

COURSE MANAGEMENT

Turn your practice into
Positive results on the Course

Good course management will decrease the amount of strokes you play on each hole.

Too many times senior golfers' will get themselves in trouble by not thinking about the shot at hand or, over-thinking the situation. The KISS principle (**K**eep **I**t **S**imple **S**eniors) should be the determining factor.

Look down the fairway or at the green. Determine where the trouble is and "play away" from it. If you hit a poor shot … forget about it! The next shot will be closer to the green.

Think positive and ask yourself is the ball advancing towards the hole? <u>If it is, you are good.</u>

Step up to the next shot, refocus, visualize your shot and begin again with the pre-shot routine.

Don't try "extra-long" shots unless you are confident that you will "get it there". It's always better to be in good shape to hit the next shot than to be in trouble or in an impossible situation.

If you find yourself in trouble, think about your options. Play a safer shot rather than risking a shot that might land you in trouble again.

Know the rules for hazards, unplayable lies, relief from trees, obstacles, cart paths, out of bounds etc. Select the applicable rule that will benefit you the most.

By playing the same course over and over we become used to "automatically" selecting the club at certain spots on the course. Think about it first and experiment with other clubs and shots. It will give you options the next time you find yourself in a similar situation.

Some Elements to Consider

- If you have to strike the ball hard to "get it there", take the next longer club, grip down approximately ¼" to ½" and swing normally. Remember that tempo and timing make for good shots – not swinging hard.

- Look at your yardages. If you don't think you can make it to the green (or a desired spot or position in the fairway) take a lesser club and swing normally to "lay the ball up" to a comfortable yardage for the next shot.

- Sidehill lies: When the ball is above your feet ... grip down a little bit. (less shaft)To keep it from "hooking" or "drawing" and take the club more upright when initiating the swing.

- Sidehill lies: When the ball is below your feet ... grip up a little bit. (more shaft) Note - never reach for a ball below your feet – bend your knees slightly (sit down) to make up for extra shaft length.

- Downhill and Uphill lies. Remember to square your shoulders to the terrain. Take a normal swing and trust your swing mechanics.

- Sand traps are no different than fairway shots. Pitch, chip, blast or putt the ball out. If there is a lip to go over – place the ball slightly forward in your stance. If there isn't a lip – consider chipping or putting the ball.

- If you find yourself in the rough – think "the ball is down ... the club goes up and then down.

Remember ..... **RELAX, BREATHE, POSITIVE ATTITUDE and ENJOYMENT are the operative words for playing golf.**

This is the philosophy that I have taught over many years of golf instruction. It is the basic premise that underlines "what will happen" throughout your golfing years.

- o Relaxation reduces the tension in your body and allows for an effortless swing.
- o Breathing promotes relaxation during the swing process.
- o Having a positive attitude encourages good shot results and limits discouragement.
- o Enjoyment is the main reason for playing golf.

Taking your game from the practice tee to the course

Remember ... <u>you always practice with a purpose.</u> Maybe it's your putting, your short game, your mid iron play, your hybrid or fairway woods and yes .... even your driver.

Visualize what you previously practiced. Think about what you worked on. Attempt to duplicate that "effortless" swing, that putting stroke, those solid iron shots going at the target and especially your driver and your "practice" fairway.

Focus on the foundations, the fundamentals of the setup and the swing. Last, but not least, relax and enjoy the game.

<u>Be grateful that you have the opportunity to play the greatest game on earth.</u>

PRACTICE DRILLS and TECHNIQUES

In this section you will find some methods
and ways to improve your game
and especially your scoring.

Always "PRACTICE WITH A PURPOSE"

It doesn't do any good to practice your faults.
Practice for improvement – know what shots will
improve your game and work on them.

Putting, chipping and pitching are at least 50%
of your score. Devote 50% of your time to
practicing this part of your game

RATING AND SLOPE: BLACK 73.5/139 GOLD 71.1/133 SILVER M 68.0/119 L 73.6/127 BRONZE M 65.2/113 L 69.9/119

HOLE	1	2	3	4	5	6	7	8	9	OUT	10	11	12	13	14	15	16	17	18	IN	TOT	HCP	NET
BLACK	390	591	442	182	400	384	489	223	444	3545	379	625	422	238	442	361	534	166	431	3598	7143		
GOLD	371	561	416	161	377	349	459	181	400	3275	358	580	398	203	385	342	511	139	399	3315	6590		
SILVER	333	511	378	130	332	320	432	154	363	2953	312	528	384	169	361	308	453	122	351	2988	5941		
BRONZE	294	474	338	96	305	291	392	116	318	2624	275	450	320	124	320	265	405	108	325	2592	5216		
HANDICAP M	13	7	3	17	11	5	1	15	9		8	6	10	16	2	12	4	18	14				
Joan	4	6	5	4	6	4	4	5	5	43	5	6	5	3	4	4	6	3	4	40	83		
(marks)	X*	X	X	*	X	X*		*	X*	6X 5*	X*	X	X*	*	X	X*	X	*	X*	7X 6*	13X 11*		
Putts	2	1	2	3	3	2	1	4	3	21	3	1	3	2	1	2	1	2	2	17	38		
Penalties		haz										ob											
PAR	4	5	4	3	4	4	5	3	4	36	4	5	4	3	4	4	5	3	4	36	72		
Doug	5	5	5	4	4	5	5	3	4	40	4	5	5	3	4	5	5	3	5	39	79		
(marks)	X*	X	X*	*	X	X*	X	*	X*	7X 6*	X*	X	X	*	X	X*	X	*	X*	6X 5*	13X 11*		
Putts	3	1	3	3	1	3	1	2	2	19	2	1	2	2	1	3	1	2	3	17	36		
Penalties																							
HANDICAP L	11	9	5	17	13	3	1	15	7		12	8	14	18	6	2	4	16	10				

MARKER _____ DATE _____

PLAYER _____

Practice for Performance and Confidence

Practice with a purpose! Don't just go to the driving range and "hit" balls. Think about what you need to improve upon and plan how you intend to accomplish it. Is it your ball striking, distance control, your short game, your setup routine, alignment, grip pressure etc. Ask yourself what are you practicing today and then do it.

Visualize your Target

Whenever you are on the range be sure to select a target to aim at. It could be a flagstick, a tree, a brown patch etc. If you are visualizing a fairway pick two points (one right and one left) and this is where you want to aim and where your ball should land.

Keeping Track on the course

The scorecard is a great way to understand what you need to work on. We seem to remember all the good shots but, what about the poor ones? What positive elements can we see in our game?

A great way to keep track of your score is to use an (X) to note a fairway hit, a (*) to indicate a green in regulation and then write down the number of putts and penalties on each hole. This will allow you to see what transpired in a round of golf and assist you in remembering what part of your game can be improved upon.

If you do this consistently, the scorecard will always tell you a story. This scorecard shows that 13 fairways were hit by each player. How about greens in regulation? How about the number of putts? What do the players need to work on to get better? Just look at the numbers!

Practice – Iron Shots

The purpose of this drill is to gain confidence in your iron play. Select three clubs. (As an example the 7, 8 and 9 iron) Begin by selecting the middle iron ... In this case the 8 iron is your focus.

Hit several shots with the 8 iron until you "feel" comfortable with the swing and the results. Hopefully you will experience that "effortless" shot during this process.

Next hit several shots with the 9 iron, then back to the 8 iron, then the 7 iron and finish with the 8 iron. Your swings should begin to feel the same.

The next time you practice ... focus on the 9 iron by selecting the pitching wedge, 9 iron and 8 irons. Repeat the same drill as before. This drill will assist you in gaining the confidence in your "repeatable" swing by using various clubs.

I do not recommend hitting the same club over and over again. You may become very comfortable with the one club but you have many club choices and you want to become more comfortable with each and every one of them.

Practice hitting your irons with a "half" swing. Develop a tempo that you can use comfortably for all your irons.

Practice hitting your irons with different ball positions and notice the differences in trajectories and distances. Forward of center higher and less distance; Rearward of center lower and more distance.

Practice – Balance and Tempo

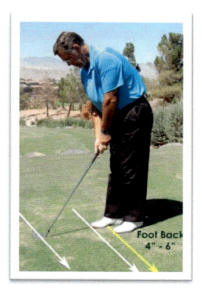

Begin with the feet together and then move the left foot back 4"-6" and swing. Feel the weight on your right side. Feel the tempo transfer the momentum to the club. Ask yourself if the swing was comfortable, balanced and relaxed. If you swing to fast you will feel off balance. If you feel the weight on your toes, you are "reaching" for the ball – stand closer.

Practice – Hip Rotation and Weight Transfer

Take a golf bag, bag stand (on the range), a chair, table or something that will rest against your hip. Simulate taking the club back and then turning your hips to face the target. The bag, chair etc. should not move. If it does … you are sliding your hips forward and the possibilities for slicing the ball or pushing it are much greater.

Practice the "Finish" Position

 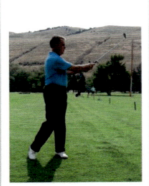 

Begin by completing your pre-shot routine and setup as if you were going to take a shot.

Place the club on the ground at the point just forward of where the club would make contact with the ball. Relax!

Now, extend your swing forward and upwards with tempo to finish in the position shown above. Your weight should be evenly distributed and balanced and your body should be in a relaxed position.

Practice your club "Takeaway"

Try placing the club approximately 4" to 8" directly behind the ball and along your swing path.

Start your backswing from this position. It will help you learn to take the club straight back and "low and slow". This drill will start the club back on the intended line and reduce the tendency to pick the club upwards too soon.

Practice – Swing Basics

Ask yourself "How can I make the swing easier and more effortless?"

(1) Think levers! Begin the backswing with your left shoulder – use the one piece take-away.

(2) Think Tempo! Slow down the backswing and make sure not to over swing – left arm should be horizontal to the ground for a full swing.

(3) Think weight transfer! Turn the hips to initiate the downswing – don't slide your hips forward – rotate them.

Practice – Pitching and Chipping

Would you be more consistent by utilizing a solid repetitive swing or modifying your swing every time you faced a shot with a different yardage?

This is an argument that has been going on throughout the ages. If you have one swing that you can master for every pitch or chip shot ... will you become more consistent and accurate by changing irons for specific yardages instead of modifying your swing?

Or, do you rely more on "feeling" the shot and using one specific club for shots of various yardages (such as a 60 degree wedge, sand iron, gap wedge etc.) then, adjusting your tempo and swing length to accommodate the shot and produce positive results.

Either method will work. Ask yourself which method is more comfortable and then perfect it by practicing. It will build confidence when utilizing the method on the course.

For the average senior golfer it sometimes makes sense to develop the one-swing and one-tempo approach. In this method you will have the same swing and tempo for every shot and only need to select the correct club given the yardage.

Begin by selecting your sand iron (56 degree). Go out to a yardage and begin hitting balls to a target. Think "half swing" and completing your follow through to the finish position as pictured previously. Adjust your yardage by moving closer or farther away until you can comfortably swing the club with almost no effort and the ball goes the desired distance.

Pace it off and write the distance down with the number of paces.

Next, select the gap wedge (52 degree) and move back 7 – 10 paces and repeat the process utilizing the same comfortable swing as before.

Continue this process with the pitching wedge and 9 irons making sure to write down the number of paces and the corresponding yardages.

When you are on the course, just pace the yardage off, refer to your "cheat sheet", select the club for that yardage and swing with confidence.

The more you use this approach the more confidence you will develop and your consistency will improve greatly.

Practice – Putting

The "3 ball" ... This drill is used for distance control and building confidence in short to middle distance putts.

Align three balls in a row. (Each ball position one club length from the previous spot)

Putt the 1st one, then the 2nd and finally the 3rd. If you miss a putt– start over!

Continue the process by moving around the hole so that you experience various putting lines, breaking points and speeds.

The "Around the Hole" ... This drill is practiced to improve accuracy, reading breaks, tempo of putter swing, speed of greens and building confidence in short to middle distance putts.

Start by placing 6 balls at one club length from the hole.

Start with one and proceed around the hole. Miss one .... Start over.

When you make all the balls ... go to 2 club lengths, then 3 club lengths etc. Miss one .... Start over.

GOLF CLUBS – What questions to ask and club considerations?

The clubs you use are an important ingredient to the success of your golf game. Many advances in the design of golf clubs have occurred over the last three decades. From the traditional forged clubs to the "revolutionary" design for cavity back clubs, adjustable drivers and fairway woods to the hybrid long irons coupled with a plethora of various types of golf shafts.

How does one select (and know) which club is best suited to their game. It is a difficult question to answer without the assistance of a professional golf fitter. It is no longer a "buy it off the rack" at a golf outlet; or purchase it from your local golf shop; or order it via the online process. The alternatives are too great.

The questions every senior golfer should be asking before making a decision on which golf clubs to use are numerous.

First, and foremost ... do you get the playability from your current clubs? How well do you hit the clubs? How solid do they feel when you strike the ball? Are they "easy" to swing? Is your accuracy what you desire? Is the distance adequate or, do you wish you had a little more? Do you know your swing speed? Do you like the look of the club? Are you satisfied with the weight of the club? Do you like the feel of your grips?

All of these factors come into play when evaluating clubs and the selections you make. Not every golfer is the same. Your choices are numerous and proper club selection will enhance your enjoyment of the game and should assist in your game improvement.

Let's start with the driver. As we age, we lose distance off the tee and fairway. This is a combination of less strength, less agility, aging muscles etc. etc. etc. How do you select the driver that is best suited to your game? Here are a few steps that will assist you.

1) Measure your current driver swing speed, launch angle and backspin on the ball with a golf professional experienced in club fitting. Write the results down.

2) Select a new driver that you like to look at. It has to be appealing to the eye to hit it well.

3) Swing it a few times and compare it to the results of the driver you presently have in your bag.

   a. How does it feel?

   b. Do you get solid contact?

   c. What is your swing speed?

   d. What is the launch angle – is it optimal?

   e. What is the "backspin" of the ball – is it too high?

   f. Are you getting additional yardage?

4) Ask your fitter about the type of shaft that best suits your game.

   a. Graphite?

   b. Senior or regular flex?

   c. Overall shaft flexibility and kick points?

   d. Weight – how many grams?

   e. Specific brands and costs – The most expensive shaft is not necessarily the best one that will improve your game.

5) Compare features of the drivers to what is currently in your bag – Is it an improvement?

    a. Adjustability – fade, draw, loft settings

    b. Length of club

    c. Warranty – if any

6) Select your driver of choice

    a. Try various shafts – select the one that optimizes your performance

        i. Distance, launch angle, limited back-spin

    b. Select your preferred grip

        i. Manufacture, type, standard or mid-size etc.

7) Last, but not least, swing the driver several times to insure that you are getting "maximum" performance that is greater than what you experience with your current driver. <u>If it is a marginal increase in performance – don't buy it</u>.

Fairway woods have always been the clubs for longer second shots to the green. As we age and our distance decreases we may, or may not, have the need for more than one fairway wood or decide to use no fairway woods at all. The development of the hybrid iron and rescue clubs has caused many seniors to go away from the traditional fairway wood to the "easier to hit" hybrids and rescues.

Ask yourself how many times in a round of golf do you hit your fairway woods. How many times were the results what you desired or expected? Could a hybrid iron or rescue club have done the job as well as the wood?

Make a decision and what combination of clubs (driver, fairway wood, and hybrid or rescue clubs) that provides the greatest benefit and most positive results for how you play the game. Select clubs that are easy to swing; select the brand that you like the looks of; select the correct shaft that maximizes your swing speed and tempo; and select a grip size that "fits your hands".

I cannot stress enough the importance of a properly fitted club. In every case, you should have the loft and lie adjusted to your swing before purchasing the clubs.

The traditional iron set containing the 3 iron to the sand wedge is no longer a viable choice for most seniors. There are many variables and each golfer's needs are different from the next. A set of irons that formerly consisted of a convential 3 and 4 iron has been replaced by hybrid 3 and 4 irons. You will find some manufacturers that have also replaced the 5 and 6 irons with hybrids. Still others have complete hybrid sets from the 3 to the 9 iron.

Iron design has also advanced over the years. Cavity back irons distribute the weight more evenly causing straighter shots when the ball is struck on the toe or heel of the club. The grooves have also been modified to reflect the changes demanded by the USGA. The steel and graphite shaft technology is far superior now than it was twenty or thirty years ago. But the most important facet of change has been the loft angle of the clubs.

Manufacturers realized that golfers would purchase newer clubs if they offered the benefit of greater distance. How does a manufacturer guarantee greater distance? It's simply a matter of physics ... decrease the loft of the club and the ball goes farther.

The pitching wedge of the past had a loft angle of 48 degrees. The "new" standard loft for the pitching wedge is approximately 44 degrees. To understand this, think of the "older" 9 iron version with a loft of 44 degrees. The new pitching wedge has the same loft of 44 degrees. Thus (in modern club sets) a 9 iron has been essentially changed into a pitching wedge thus creating greater distances with the shorter iron.

Iron set considerations are the same as items 1 – 7 as previously discussed in the driver section. Appearance, manufacturer, forged or cast club heads, graphite or steel shafts and grip type and style are additional considerations.

Understand the differences between forged and cast club heads. Cavity back irons in today's environment offer the greatest distance, accuracy, durability and forgiveness sacrificing the option of "working" the ball from left to right (fade for a right hander) and right to left (draw for a right hander) in most cases.

The overwhelming choice and recommendation for senior golfers playing the game today is a cavity back iron with either a regular graphite or senior graphite shaft and hybrid irons that complement the set.

This can be a difficult decision to make for most amateur senior golfers. Here you will make a decision based on how the club "feels" when you swing it. If it feels really good, you will have a tendency to purchase it on the spot.

Let me warn you about an impulse decision when purchasing a single club or a complete set of irons. Always compare any new club with the clubs presently in your bag. Ask what the swing weight is for the club;

ask about the shaft weight, composition, flex points, stiff tip etc. and length prior to making a decision to purchase. All of these factors contribute to how a club "feels" to you.

Make sure you try different combinations of shafts and club heads until you reach the "perfect" club that maximizes your swing tempo and playing ability. Do <u>not</u> be sold a "standard" set of clubs (off the rack) without exploring club head and shaft alternatives that are available to you.

Last, but not least, do not purchase a new set of irons without having them adjusted for your swing. Insure that the lofts and lies are correct for your swing.

If the retailer says they can't adjust them – find another store that will. Do not purchase anything that is not optimal for your game.

DEFINITIONS
and
REVIEW NOTES

DEFINITIONS:

HEEL SHOT – a point at which the ball contacts the clubface closer to the hosel on the clubface.

TOE SHOT – the point at which the ball contacts the clubface closer to the outside point of the clubface

FAT SHOT – that "chunky" feeling when the clubface enters the ground too far behind the ball

SKINNY SHOT – that "hard" feeling when you hit the ball instead of the impacting the ground.

CLUB (LOFT) – the angle of the clubface relative to a flat surface. The shorter the iron the more loft.

CLUB (LIE) – the angle of the clubface to the shaft when the clubhead is setting on a flat surface.

CLUB (LAUNCH ANGLE) – the angle at which a ball leaves the clubface relative to a flat surface.

CLUB (SWINGWEIGHT) – a measurement used to indicate the "feel and weight of the club"

SWING TEMPO – the speed at which the body relates to the swinging of the club.

GRIPs (TYPES) – There are numerous manufacturers of composite and rubber grips on the market. They come in standard, midsize, large and specialty grips for putters etc. Select the one that "feel" good to you.

- o GRIP (OVERLAP) – a grip where the baby finger on one hand is placed overlapping the index and second finger of the opposite hand.

- o GRIP (INTERLOCKED) - a grip where the baby finger on one hand is placed between the index and second finger of the opposite hand.

- o GRIP (ten finger)) – a grip (sometimes referred to as a baseball grip) where all fingers come in contact with the club.

SHAFT (GRAPHITE) – a composite shaft for woods or irons designed to provide maximum playability for various types of clubs and golfers skill levels. This type of shaft is recommended for most senior golfers.

SHAFT (STEEL) – as the name implies, a steel shaft that has been used for ages prior to the development of the graphite shaft. Better golfers with lower handicaps will generally use this shaft in their irons.

SHAFT (KICK POINT) – each shaft will flex differently depending upon the design. A "higher" kickpoint provides increased speed and "whip" at the point of impact with the ball. The slower the swing speed the higher the kickpoint.

SHAFT (FLEX) – regular, firm, stiff, senior, ladies shafts have all different shaft flexes. The difference is how much they weigh and how much they bend (flex) during the swing process.

DRIVER (ADJUSTMENTS) – technology has changed the look and feel of many clubs. Loft angle, launch angle, backspin, fade or draw adjustments are now very common. Choose the one that best suits your game.

Review Notes:

Every good golf swing begins with preparation.

1) Basic pre-shot routine
   a. Clubface centered behind the ball
   b. Correct posture (Bow to the Queen)
   c. Relaxed Grip
   d. Stance and ball position correct
2) The full swing
   a. The take-away
      i. Swing Path (Straight back and then up)
      ii. Direction (backwards and low to the ground)
      iii. Tempo (smooth and controlled)
   b. The turn
      i. How much – Slightly
      ii. Is it necessary – Depends on Player
   c. The position at the top
      i. The wrist break - Limited
      ii. The arm position – Horizontal with the ground
   d. The first move in the Downswing
      i. Hips - Always
      ii. Elbow – Collapses to side
   e. The impact position
      i. Square - Preferred

        ii. Open – Goes right

       iii. Closed – Goes left

   f. The follow through – Finish by looking at your target

3) The ball flight and direction – Ball position, loft of club and clubface at impact

4) Pitching and chipping – Always finish by pointing the club at your target

5) Sand shots – "spank" the sand – club up – club down

6) Putting – Low and Slow … right hand in the hole

7) Sidehill lies/uphill lies/downhill lies – Don't like these … see drills

8) The mental side of the game – Have only one swing thought at a time

Conclusions:

Remember why you play the game. Enjoy it with your friends and family.

Play the game for fun. If it isn't fun anymore …. Stop playing, take a break and come back to it later.

Better yet … when you do begin to play again, contact a local PGA teaching professional who will assist you in getting better and enjoying the game again.

ABOUT the AUTHOR:

Gary J. Lee is a PGA teaching professional who has over thirty years of golf instruction and coaching experience.

He has coached and instructed both men and women players of all ages and abilities. Junior players, high school and collegiate teams, mini - tour players, adults and senior golfers.

Gary is currently a teaching professional, personal coach and instructor at the Revere Golf Club in Henderson, Nevada.

His teaching expertise and knowledge of the game extends beyond daily lessons and clinics. Gary has mentored aspiring PGA apprentices in all facets of golf instruction, club fitting, on course management and the principles for lower scoring.

It has been said that his teaching style is easy and simple to understand. You can judge for yourself after reading the contents of this book.